MW01125959

Writing & Design : Pauline Lejust

Inquiries : dsignbypauline@gmail.com

Youtube & Instagram : Pauline Lejust

Dear readers.

This book is the continuation of the first book "Manifest it with Quantum Physics". If you don't understand or have forgotten certain principles, we invite you to read or reread the first book. The principle of repetition makes it possible to memorize information consciously and subconsciously. That's why so many people read and reread the same books. Oftentimes people say that information is repeated, the turn of sentences is changed, or that certain principles are copied from book to book, author to author. It's the case. People share the same ideas and concepts because they reach the same goals : make of this world a more joyful place to live in, for everyone.

Table of Contents

CHAPTER ONE

THE MATRIX

1. QUANTUM PHYSICS

It's a science that describes that all things created are coming to a perceived existence. The human body is created from cells, blood and *matter*. All these particles form something that creates our solidity, our "physical form". Every single part of you, every cell, and bone are created from the basic ingredients of *quantum particles* (atoms, neutrons, protons, electrons which are the building blocks of all matter). Everything you see around you these particles: the air, your thoughts, the animals, nature, your car, the objects. *Everything is made of quantum particles.* Everything we see was created by the Universe and there are 4 fundamental forces that govern things:

◇ GRAVITY

◇ THE WEAK FORCE

◇ ELECTROMAGNETISM

◇ THE STRONG FORCE

One of them is the *electromagnetic spectrum.* There is weak nuclear force and strong nuclear force in gravity. The weak is responsible for radioactive decay, the strong is the component, "the glue" that holds all these particles together. Gravity is the force that pulls things together, it always attracts. Gravity is the law of attraction. There are frequencies and chemicals that your brain produces that the law of attraction is addicted to. It's a very powerful chemical that turns into a magnetic frequency known as the *electromagnetic frequency. If you know how to use and tune into this frequency, you can attract everything you desire.*

2. THE LAW OF ATTRACTION

The Law of Attraction is the belief that positive or negative thinking brings positive or negative experiences into a person's life. In simple terms, *the Law of Attraction* is the ability to attract into our lives whatever we are focusing on. It's using the power of the mind to translate whatever is in our thoughts and materialize them into reality. A key component of the philosophy is that in order to effectively change one's negative thinking patterns, one must also "feel" (through creative visualization) that the desired changes have already occurred. This combination of positive thought and positive emotion is believed to allow one to attract positive experiences and opportunities by achieving resonance with the proposed energetic law.

Law of attraction is a gravitational force coupled with a part of the electromagnetic spectrum (electricity and magnetism). It's a constant force always pulling towards quantum particles. You and I are all created by these based particles. Let's make sure you understand. Take the example of baking; When you bake a cake, you need to put the ingredients (sugar, spices, flour..) together to create your cake. Quantum particles are like ingredients but they are invisible to the human eye, they are energy based. *How can something that seems real be created from some*thing that isn't real? In a physical sense?

Humans, animals, and every single thing that you witness in the Universe is comprised and made from these particles.

How does this interact with the Universal principles? The fundamental forces that govern are responsible for the activity of these particles. The consciousness is also commanding and they listen to your thoughts. Your thoughts carry vibrational energy, and this energy will create and attract.

We live in an attraction-based universe. **Everything is attracted to us**, which means the good and the bad. What you focus your thoughts on, comes back to you. You can attract the things that you want but also the things that you don't want. What you focus on, you will attract. Always. It can be proved in physics with the *observer effect (the fact that observing a situation or phenomenon necessarily changes it)*: quantum particles exist in a state called "duality". If you are not thinking or observing something, in physics it doesn't exist and it's not there, but the minute you turn your attention on that thing/subject, it actually starts to materialize, creating this particle and coming into existence.

You actually control your mind and thoughts, they bring things into existence. The power source of the law of attraction is your mind, your consciousness. Your mind emits particles, they have intelligence and obey you. A particle will be "at rest" until it gets a command, coming from your consciousness. The moment you start to think of a car or something that you desire, that particle will start to materialize. Remember that everything that you want already exists, the wealth, the car, the money, the abundance, the happiness, etc. It's already out there. All you have to do is to create the matching frequency, by continuously focusing on your desires.

3. REALITY

Your mind is a very powerful tool and has the unique capability to process thoughts. Without thoughts, nothing exists. Your thoughts create energy which creates vibration, and vibration creates reality. The brain works through repetition. The neural pathway creates neuron cells and they adapt to your belief system. A belief is something that you hold to be true within your consciousness. Consciousness is awareness about who you are and your identity. It has a direct result on your reality. **Who are you?** You are a powerful being, you are so much more than what you perceive yourself to be. Within you exists a "spiritual dimensional being" (something beyond the physical: gut feeling, intuition, the voice in your head). Reality is a perception. *The observer effect* shows that what you focus on is coming into existence. Your reality is based on your perception. Your thoughts and your beliefs interact and become what is called "reality". Something that you perceive that is real.

You will probably think that if these particles are invisible to the naked eye, **how can they be real?** How can we, the car, the objects surrounding us be real? In reality, there is no solidity. An atom is 99% empty space. You and I and everything in this Universe is made from atoms.

So, how can things be and feel physically real? Let's talk about atoms. Every single thing is composed of these particles: atoms in your body, a chair, a phone, a tree. Within each particle is a kind of repelling force between the positive and the negative charges. When you are touching or feeling something, your brain is sending a signal to the neurons, your brain interprets this signal. If you touch an object, the particles in your hand and within the object are repeling each other (- +) and you feel the repulsion of

2 magnetic signals. In reality, you are never touching anything or never sitting in a car, you are always "levitating".

If the Universe decides to turn off one of these 4 fundamental forces, the reality will change. For example, if the electromagnetic force is turned off, if you touch a table, your finger is going through the table. That means reality is an illusion of perception for your brain. Your brain is a receiver, it receives information from your *consciousness* which is your authentic you, and it interacts within your reality to create and attract.

It shows you that you are powerful. Your thoughts bind and create all these universal concepts. Every single thing that you are witnessing or attracted to you, is created through your thoughts. Your thoughts have energy.

4. HOW DOES REALITY WORK WITH THE LOTTERY?

The one thing that the Universe uses to translate anything is numbers.

It's all about mathematics, and it wasn't something we've invented, but something we discovered. Numbers will pop up for you and you don't have to look for them. *Oh, and you'll probably got crazy at the beginning then you'll get used to it.*

Here are some examples of angel numbers

111 : Self-trust. Your intentions are manifesting very quickly. Make sure you are focusing on what you want.

222 : Balance, seeds, collaboration. **Stop worrying, everything is working out just as it's supposed to. You are on the right path.**

333 : Divine flow. **Ascendant masters are assisting you, you're in great hands.**

444 : Manifestation, grounding. **You are completely surrounded by angels and you're being guided through whatever you're focusing on.**

555 : Change. **Huge positive changes. Trust that this transition is for your highest good. Prepare for massive shifts.**

666 : Surrender. **Your thoughts need some refocusing. Remember that you are a spiritual being having a human experience. Reconnect with your spirituality.**

777 : Evolution, wisdom, luck is on your side. **You are on the ultimate path, keep doing what you are doing.**

888 : Flow, power, abundance. **Lots of money. You are aligned with the money you desire.**

999 : Culmination. **You're being nudged to finish something because that completion will unlock the next step for you.**

1111 : Instant manifestation. **You are on the right path. You're a Master manifestor and know exactly where you're going. Alignment.**

OOO : New beginnings, a fresh start. **Being one with the Universe. Remember that you are the creator of your destiny.**

The way reality works is, you hear about odds, the chances, and the probabilities. When you pursue a ticket, they have the odds on it (*the mega-million will say one chance in a hundred million.* We have a stigma about the lottery which is conditioned into our minds. "*The lottery is gambling*", "*Only poor people play*", "*You are never going to win*", "*It's a scam*", "*It's too hard*", "*It's a game of chance*". We are all familiar with these sayings, just like we hear that "*money is the root of all evil*".

The big thing is that these sayings are an interpretation and a perception from us. Everything you see in your life right now is always in two parts at the same time, but you can't see them because your brain can only focus on one thing at a time. The mind can't focus on two things at once.

Reality exists in a state of probability, which is **anything can happen.** The chances are *called the waves in quantum physics*, all possible outcomes exist right there. This what it's called superposition. It's a frozen state.

Reality exists in what's called actuality, which is going from probability (just one of the two options) and it becomes your actual reality. *Let's take an example with 2 people.*

✧ Person A = *"the lottery is a game of chance, so I go into the probability Universe and I take the game of chance and I bring it into my actual unit reaction"*. The mindset of person A is focused on chance, meaning *"I won't win"*.

✧ Person B = *"I'm going to win the lottery, it's not a game of chance for me, this is something I'm going to deliberately create. Now I go to the probability Universe, remembering I have all options now, the Universe gives me the actuality of me winning the game".*

Person B changed his mindset. Now, he doesn't look at the lottery as gambling, chance, or probability. Take one of the options and make it possible: possibility > actuality. Each person has access to these realities at the same time. Every person has that. It's our own unique interpretation of possibility that will separate you from the other person.

Now you realize that the lottery isn't a game of chance, you see the lottery as a game of possibility and actuality. Our physical world is actually kind of like a game, almost a video game, all options are available. Nothing in the physical world is impossible. The only impossibility is our minds creating the limits. You don't have a limitless mind, you only have limited beliefs. When you play the lottery, you can actually change it from a game of chance to a winning game, to a deliberate creation of anything.

CHAPTER TWO

VALUABLE ADVICE

1. THE IMPORTANCE OF MEDITATION

Meditation is the gate to your deepest desires and access to the quantum realm.

MEDITATION is the most powerful form of communication with your subconscious mind and directly connects you with your higher self. This practice should be taught at school : it can relieve stress, increase energy, cure illness. It is also a portal. It sets the tone for you to know your higher self. It brings inspired action. It gives you knowledge, vision, the "aha moment", and information to create. The key to meditation is to silence the mind, be in a state of feeling your body language: your breathing. To meditate, make sure there is no distraction (phone and tv off), and choose a nice quiet relaxed space. You need to relax. Close your eyes, take a deep breath, and focus on breathing in and out for 4 minutes. We are distracting the ego-mind in two ways: breathing and observing your breathing. Once you are able to do that, you have pure bliss, no thoughts, *now you are meditating.*

In these stages of meditation, your higher self comes in intuition, enlightenment, insight. The answers will be revealed through meditation.

Your intuition gets heightened and becomes more knowledgeable. When you meditate nothing incredible happens, you just feel nice and peaceful. When you get out of this meditation, your higher self has already downloaded the information that you have been desiring and, it gets stored into the subconscious mind. So when the time is right for you to hack, booom it appears! You have the right nudges. You do the right thing at the right time. You have more confidence and you'll be more enlightened because now you have established a connection. I personally meditate 3 times a day but you can have your own rhythm.

VISUALIZATION is the art of putting images in the mind and it creates your reality.

REPETITION is the key, imagine the same image or situation again and again. The more vivid, the more you repeat it, the faster the subconscious will accept it. And it will become a reality. The mind will create and shape it for you.

VIVIDNESS

Put details, the colors, the shape, the feeling of having it, the design, the home, the car, the relationship, the job, the travel trip... it must be in a state of normality. Visualize as if you deserve it and you're supposed to have it. That puts you in alignment with the subconscious mind, when you see things in a state of normality it creates the outcome faster. Why? Because the subconscious mind exists in a state of normality, it doesn't get impressed. It has the power to create anything. However, the conscious mind gets impressed with fantasies. When you visualize, avoid manifesting into a fantasy format because it's the ego mindset. Visualize as if it's the next logical step. You are supposed to have it. It's normal and there is nothing spectacular. It's supposed to happen. When you do that, the subconscious mind has the vibrational frequency of normality and thinks *"ok, let's give it more of this"*.

Why not? Because the Universe exists for you to have whatever you desire. There is abundance enough for everyone on this planet. It's your birthright.

> *Be like the sun. You know it's going to rise every morning. You don't need to go around and check if the sun comes up. It's normal and natural. It's the same for the desires of your heart. They will be met.*

EMOTIONS

When you visualize anything that you desire, your mind will follow your emotions. If it's something you like or something you want, you're automatically going to feel good. The mind will do it naturally because it is something that you desire and that makes you feel good.

2. LEARN TO TRAP YOUR CONSCIOUS MIND

How to make the conscious mind believe it's not a game of chance or gambling?

SEE THE LOTTERY AS AN INVESTMENT

People invest in the stock market and cryptocurrency and nobody says gambling if you put money on stocks. They call it an investment. Get used to seeing the lottery as an investment, you put your money in, you expect to get something back. Now your conscious and subconscious mind has kind of the same agreement. Aligning both of your minds is the key to manifestation. You have the awareness to know what you want and tell your mind. That's how you manifest.

WITH YOUR SUBCONSCIOUS MIND

It works with old programming from childhood. There is a battle between the conscious & the subconscious, and that creates resistance. Resistance is when you have a difficult time getting what you want. You put so much energy and so much work that you get tired and when you get it, it doesn't last. The subconscious is sabotaging the conscious and they create this resistance. The subconscious wins most of the time because it's a powerful source that controls your actions and your habits.

In our minds, we make it complex. The information is very complex but, it's really simple. Life can be easy if you let it be easy. Your paradigm (the way of looking at something) is your belief structure and you need to change it. With the lottery, see your mind moving forward and say to yourself *"This lottery is my investment, it's a process of creation, it's not a game of luck or chances. I deliberately create my own luck. I deliberately created it to win the lottery"*.

> When they created the lottery market, they knew the reality most people lived in: it's a game of luck, this is why they are able to get so many players. The lottery is winning more people because these people are playing with the mindset of luck or chance. That's why the lottery market always puts the odds into our heads to get more profits. There are not going to tell you the truth. They probably don't even know themselves that you can deliberately create your win, or if they do they probably know that only a few have "the secret"? But they don't care because the majority of the masses are trying to win and buy.

~~DON'T *TRY TO*~~ WIN THE LOTTERY

When you try something, you are lying to yourself. Trying is lying. When you try, the Universe and the subconscious mind try back. When you put the word try into the Universe your subconscious freezes your mind and you become stuck. Your subconscious mind says trying doesn't give any results. If you want something you have to do so! You don't try something. You just do it.

Change your words and mindset in order to manifest and change all areas of your life. When you go to play the lottery, never have the mindset *"I'm going to try to win. I'm just going to keep playing and trying."*. Choose instead *"I'm going to repeat the process until I get my desired results."*

YOUR SUBCONSCIOUS MIND IS GULLIBLE

It is easily taken in or tricked. You can compare it to the mind of a child, he can believe in unicorns and magic. The only difference for an adult is the ability to create. The words and language we use in our regular mind, we think and we know what it means to us. Trying means eventually doing it until I get it right but not for your subconscious mind. But in reality trying is lying so you are lying to your mind and to yourself.

BE A VIBRATIONAL MATCH

If you start to look at your mindset like looking for matching numbers it's going to be debilitating. You see it as a BIG challenge. By saying "OMG I just missed just one number" you put yourself in the *trying world*. Don't look at your numbers. They don't matter. What you are looking for is a vibrational match. When you win the numbers, they will match up vibrationally. Winning the lottery isn't about winning numbers. Winning the lottery is matching the frequency. Being in the right place at the right time, you are going to buy the right quick pick, which is perfect timing and it's going to match.

YOU ARE AT THE RIGHT PLACE AT THE RIGHT TIME

Your mantra is: *Why am I consistently in the right place at the right time, winning top-tier lottery jackpot prizes?* Your subconscious mind is going to start to move and shake. It's going to give you an intuition to go to this store before you go to bed. You might get an image of another store, or you may be driving and all of a sudden you get an urge to stop at *that* store. That's because you are impressing it and it's going to put you in the right place. You go into a store to buy your regular ticket. You get a scratch off. This ticket just stands out to you. Buy the ticket. Don't question it. Don't think *"don't do that!". Just feel it.* Tap into your intuition and what your body tells you. If you don't feel it, don't force anything.

SET UP A SYSTEM

You are a deliberate creator but it's all about personal work. You have to change your mindset radically. Prepare yourself. Get rid of the past. Have consistency, faith, discipline and repeat the process. If you put the work with consistency, your mind believes you more when you take action. First, you need to decide and choose how much do you want to win, and then you're going to create a daily system.

3. IT'S TIME TO TAKE ACTION

Money will not come physically into your life if you don't put the physical effort.

CREATE A BUDGET

This is an investment. Determine how much money you can play weekly, including the money you can afford to what you might call "lose". The fantasy five plays every day. The Powerball and the Mega play twice a week, so you have to decide what you can afford. My advice is to buy 2, 5 tickets per week.

BUY YOUR TICKETS PHYSICALLY

If you travel a lot, you can do advanced play. If you are in the state you want to physically go out and buy your tickets, this way you're mapping your reality and it contributes additional, vivid images for your subconscious mind. It's also more fun, the lottery is an extension to give you extra abundance. It's your birthright to enjoy the process. It helps you build your intuition. You can always pick up energy, choose a place to buy your tickets only if you feel good energy about it.

KEEP YOUR TICKETS IN A SAFE PLACE

Stay organized and consider your tickets as something valuable, so find a safe document case to put your tickets inside. You don't put anything in a safe that isn't valuable, right? When you buy your tickets, the subconscious mind is watching you (remember it's illogical) and one of these tickets must become a valuable winner. You are convincing your mind that this ticket you are putting in the safe, you're going to make it a winner. It's going to put you at the right place at the right time to match its interpretation of a valuable thing.

CRYSTALS

I call them enhancers. They have a very conductive energy material. The way they are made, they can channel energy. All your electronic devices. Liquid quartz or LCD (Liquid Crystal Display) is a type of flat panel display which uses liquid crystals in its primary form of operation. They can be commonly found in smartphones, televisions, computer monitors, and instrument panels. If the crystals weren't part of our Universe, none of our electronic equipment could work because they would overheat. The reason why your phone doesn't explode on you, it's because when the energy comes in the crystals take the energy and isolate it out. It's efficient. It takes energy and it runs it smoothly. You have different types of crystals: for psychic abilities, to increase your vibrations, to make you happy, so you can dream more, to control your mood, to bring money and luck.

Buy a Green Aventurine. Buy a couple and put them in your safe. It's going to help to raise the vibration. When you go buy your tickets, play your numbers quick picks and listen to the voice telling you what to play. Buy 2,3,4 or 5 tickets because it brings you a higher vibration to create more abundance so don't think too much.

YOUR INTUITION IS YOUR BEST FRIEND

Go buy your tickets and when you are finished take a quick look at all the scratch-offs, and if one of them calls your name, buy it. There may be something about the ticket that draws you to it. Don't lose yourself in the ego-mind and the logical part. There will be some days when your intuition will tell you to go there, and others days when

you'll not get anything. If one ticket particularly is attracting you, don't look at the price, just buy it. At the end of the month, you can check your tickets.

CLAIM YOUR TICKET

By signing the back of your ticket, it's a powerful message for your subconscious mind. When you sign something, what does it mean? It's official. It's your validation. It's yours. At the lottery they will not cash your prize until you sign it. It's the same process with the subconscious. Every time you get home you want to turn it over and endorse the back of the ticket because you are expecting to win.

Remember that you are creating this. Treat your ticket as a winner and give it values and protection, that way it shows to the subconscious that...it's real. When you have jewelry and money in your house, you keep them in a pretty case or box, not on the table or in a vase-like any receipt. *Lottery tickets are uncashed checks.* They are ready to be manifested in something abundant and huge. When you are expecting something you must be sure that you will have it as, *opposed to being needy (which is creepy energy) and you're obsessed with the "how" and "when".* When you need something it puts pressure on you and your mind and creates resistance and lack.

WE ARE ALL WINNERS

Why you don't win? You put too much power on the lottery, you put it on a pedestal. The lottery is an extra abundance. It's a part of you and your equivalence, it's not superior to you. The majority of people play because they need it, not for fun and enjoying the process. They need to win and it creates resistance. That's why the lottery targets low-income people because they know *that dream* to win millions of dollars. When someone doesn't have the money and is trying to spend their last rent money to play the lottery because they see this dream. That's why it was designed: to target your subconscious. People are making winning the lottery difficult by getting in a state of mood, stress, and doubt. The majority of the winners weren't in desperate need of winning the lottery, they weren't obsessed with it. Some of them even lost their tickets in their house and found them months later. They completely forgot ! (Detachment). Many of them were playing just for fun.

4. MANIFEST FASTER

You are doing a quantum leap.

Focus on:

Visualizing on the lottery winnings 30%

Meditate on the winnings and afterward 70%

The lottery is a tool to gain what you desire. When you close your eyes you will visualize yourself walking into the lottery office with the ticket and there is a lady at the front and she is telling you "*Congratulations!*". You give her your ticket with a smile. She scans your ticket and right above you there is a screen saying *TOP PRIZE WINNER*. Put the amount of money you would like to see on it. (You choose your number).

What would you like to do with the money? Pay your debts, buy your dream house, your dream car, invest. Visualize the freedom, unlimited abundance, your house, the floors, the rooms, the design, the plants, the colors, shapes, and style, same with your car. Be as specific as you can.

USE MUSIC

I use my favorite meditational music. Music amplifies your vibration, makes you more magnetic. You manifest a lot faster.

MAKE THE LOTTERY SMALL AND NORMAL

During the daytime, you are more focused on what you want and what you do with the lottery. But now you do it from a non-attachment point, you have a nice balance. Remember what I said about how to view the lottery? It's an investment. You are not trying to win the lottery, you are just repeating the process until you get your desired results! Know that we live in two realities simultaneously:

✧ we have one reality called *"actuality"*: the things you see right now, confidence, trust, see the lottery as an investment

✧ we have another reality called *"possibility"*: probabilities, doubt, slow

In order to do that, take actions: go physically buy the ticket, put it in the safe. That's going to create a habit and make it "normal", easy. The lottery is fun. It's an investment that is helping me. I love seeing this, and I love what the Universe can bring to me in possibilities. You continue to do that. Make it a habit. Repeat.

BUILD YOUR INTUITION

Scratch game tips. Portfolio games, called Scratch-offs come in different price ranges: $1 to $50. You can win between $10 and $50 millions dollars instantly on the bigger games. Your higher self and the Universe know the winning tickets because each winning ticket vibrates on a special frequency. Remember, if something has money on it it's going to vibrate differently as something that doesn't have money. You're going to feel the winning tickets, and that's what I'm going to teach you to pick up on.

When you go to the store :

- ✧ look at the glass where the scratch-offs are
- ✧ take a nice deep breath
- ✧ glance at the tickets
- ✧ but don't stare at them
- ✧ one ticket will call you, listen to your intuition
- ✧ buy it !!!
- ✧ you don't care about the price
- ✧ you can't explain why it's this ticket

DISCOVER THE RESULT

After you take it home, put it in the safe. Or you can scratch it and see the results. You can scan the bar code. What I personally do at the end of every month, I take all my tickets and, I physically go into the store because I really love the experience, I just love to go in there and embody and have fun. When I first won that experience was what helped me create a visual image. That's how I would visualize at night because I could see myself in a particular store, scanning all I want. You can download on play store a lottery app on your phone. You can do it from your house too if you feel comfortable doing it virtually.

PART THREE

WORK ON YOURSELF

1. DISCIPLINE AND CONSISTENCY

Habits and rituals are a routine that gets your mind into attracting your desires.

GRATITUDE

Be grateful for what you currently have to stay in the same frequency energy. *Example: "Thank you for this nice house I have. Thank you for my health. Thank you for my family and tribe."* **Be grateful for what you intend to have in the present moment as if you already have it now.** *Example: "Thank you for my promotion, for my brand new car, for my five bedroom home (if you have a three bedroom home), for my new moto".*

You want to expand your gratitude and reach for your true desires. The trick with the subconscious mind is that it doesn't know the difference between what you have and what you want ;). Nor does your subconscious know the difference between reality and imagination. If you give gratitude for what you have and what you're reaching for, it's going to produce that. Like the Bible said, what you ask for, if you believe that it is already yours, you should have it. Everything works in frequency and vibration so give gratitude for what you intend to manifest as if you have it. The only limit is the ego, it will

21

come and distract you, but now you know how to disregard that mind and disengage it.

Gratitude is one of the most powerful sources that we can access to create your reality. Why? The power and frequency of gratitude exists in a high dimension plane. It vibrates with love, empathy and forgiveness. It's a very powerful, highly energetic magnetic force. Once you can use gratitude on a daily basis and you start to accept what you have been visualizing, it shifts you and your universe and creates a whole new realm of possibilities.

AFFIRMATIONS

Alpha theta frequencies every night. They will operate in the range to build abundance, prosperity, or any part of your life you want to manifest. You sleep with them every night, you give gratitude, go to sleep and listen to these frequencies. When you are about to fall asleep, you can use the **why technique.** You can say to yourself *why am I so abundant, why do I have so much money in my bank account, why is it so easy for me to manifest money, why am I so healthy and strong.* When you are falling asleep, you are entering into that trans state.

DAILY ROUTINE

✧ *A glass of water.* When you wake up, drink a glass of water. It cleans your body and energy and prepares you for the day.

✧ *Mirror.* When you go to the bathroom after the cold shower, use the Why Technique in front of your mirror. Self-reflection combined with affirmations is a powerful tool. You manifest faster.

- ✧ *During the day.* Control your thoughts and change them if you notice the ego-mind playing with you. You basically can shake your head, and say "back off" to the ego mind. Focus only on your desires.

- ✧ *Meditation.* 5, 10, 15 minutes a day, when you are relaxed and in a peaceful environment.

- ✧ *Gratitude.* Again, you say it out loud or you can write it.

BE PATIENT AND PERSISTENT

You can't discourage easily. When you lose a ticket, it's just that your manifestation hasn't occurred yet. Your ego is limited and looks for time and wants visible results, but your mind can't see. Remember about the time theory. You can't be in the mindset of time like months and years. You just have to be present and just play until you get the desired result.

DON'T . THINK . ABOUT . THE . WHEN.

That's irrelevant because your subconscious mind can't see the time. Your ego does, it's limited. It's looking for time. You have to bypass the concept of time, days, weeks, months, years. Again, your mind can't see. You have to play until the desired results.

Most of the time your ego can discourage you to do something. It's fear and it's not real. Fear doesn't exist, it's your mind playing against you. It's a kind of self-sabotage. A part of you makes you feel like something is wrong if you win, something is wrong if you are happy or feel good, something is wrong if you succeed. Sometimes people are living such a good moment that they are expecting the fall, the situation turning out against them, they auto-sabotage. There is no one who has the power to ruin your life or moments, except you.

Yes, God is not punishing you, nor the Universe, nor Tim from 4th grade, nor your teacher from high school, nor your ex, nor your coworkers, nor your boss, nor your mother-in-law , nor your neighbors. You are the one sabotaging your life.

No one, absolutely no one, and nothing has power over your life, except you.

It took me over a year to first manifest my big win. Because of limited beliefs, subconscious blockages, and access to this state of 100% trust in myself. At first, I was obsessed with the notion of time, then I started to detach. When I won, it happened at the perfect time. It didn't feel like a year. Trust me, it was worth the wait. Oh, and by the way, there is no wait. Timing is a human invention. That's the mindset you need, the winning one, the 100% confidence and trust in yourself.

2. FEELING IS THE SECRET

Feel and experience high-frequency emotions in your body to manifest faster.

HAVE FUN AND PLAY

Ask yourself: *if I am diligent and, I play for one year on a daily basis, can I win two million dollars?* Well...hell yeah! That's a nice investment, right? And a fun one. Playing the lottery or investing in bitcoins or the stock market is exactly the same, this is the same energy, and you reach the same goal: freedom. If you give, you will receive, that's a natural law. Playing the lottery is fun, but investing too. You have to play and have fun! Know that the secret is feeling, everything is related to your emotions and how you feel. *If you play when you are needy, stressed, anxious, desperate or have scarcity moments, don't do it.* You have to play when you have a high-vibe frequency, when you feel joyful, when you feel good, and when you have trust. You can't be an instant millionaire. That's a trap you need to avoid. It positions you on a desperate and needy frequency. And guess what, it repels. You are playing the lottery as a secondary option from the Universe to give you what you want.

BE JOYFUL

Winning the lottery will never give you love, friends, or happiness, forget about that. This is something you have to build, all by yourself. Any work, any task in your daily life should be fun too. Even the personal tasks at home: groceries, cleaning, taking care of the kids, the dogs. You should feel and experience joy on a daily basis, especially in small things. This is the secret to manifestations, feel what emotions the lottery brings you, feel the emotions and the freedom of winning the lottery. How does it feel? You feel free, you feel helped, you feel safe.

The feeling of joy we are constantly talking about, that sparkle, it's all about being grateful. Gratitude can be expressed through many forms and feeling pure joy, happiness or excitement is a way to energetically say "thank you" and share your gratitude, give yourself a good moment. You can be grateful silently, saying it out loud, screaming it, writing it, dancing it, shaking it, driving it (carefully), cooking it! Whatever is your personal and unique expression mode for gratitude, the more joy you'll experience, the more you will manifest.

UNDERSTAND YOUR EMOTIONS

Scarcity doesn't exist in nature. There is always abundance out there. *Scarcity was invented by humans*, and we've been conditioned to be afraid of "lacking" since we were born. But that's a lie. We live in a consumer society, a capitalist world, and everything is done and calculated to make you want more and to possess more.

Have you uncovered the emotions behind your intentions? You don't want to win the lottery, you are not looking for the virtual money in you bank account. You actually want to experience the feeeeeeling that this manifestation will bring you. People don't realize that but they are actually looking for the emotions that the possessions will bring them. Which emotions they will experience: freedom, love, appreciation, passion, fulfillment, joy, empowerment? Uncover and embody those emotions as often as possible, when you do this you become a vibrational match and a magnet for your desires.

RETURN ON INVESTMENT

When you play the lottery, it's for fun. When you invest and buy a ticket, you can lose one dollar, or you can win a million dollars. That's worth the investment, the top prize is worth it, the second prize too. You can win cash, free food, $500, $100, $50, $10, you can win the prizes in between, it's still abundance, it's still money, and you are still winning the lottery no matter how much you won. There is no difference between $1 and $1 million...it's the same frequency. Even if you win another ticket, it's still a won. Don't underestimate the power of a free ticket because this is abundance. Remember it's energy and the Universe is testing your level of commitment and appreciation.

If you reject or complain about the small wins, what message are you sending to the Universe? That this amount is too small? It's not enough? First, you repel all forms of abundance. Then you will never have enough if this is your current mindset. *It is crucial for you to know how to appreciate the small victories in your daily life. The more you show gratitude and experience joy, the more you will be able to enjoy your moments – all of them – the more the Universe will give to you. That's why we say "like attract like". A win is still a win, no matter the value, no matter the amount or the quantity. The more grateful you are, the more joyful you will experience your winnings, the more you will receive. Be intentionally and truly thankful for what you have, you'll attract more.*

It happened to me many time. I was doing the opposite when I would win. I had reactions like "Oh man, a free ticket uh, $2 seriously, come on I need big money". And it feels off, I just stopped winning and there was resistance. So, I reversed the situation, tuned in, and start to be grateful for everything. I was saying a huge yes when they were offering me a free ticket. And I was winning even more!

A winning ticket is winning the lottery. You want to win a substantial amount or win the jackpot. And that's what you want to convince your mind: you are winning the lottery. When you are grateful for every win, the small wins become big wins. Everything goes in multiplication, everything is constantly growing and expanding. The Universe is looking for something that makes you feel good, and you are telling the Universe money wins, so what the Universe does: it sends all these things to you in a multiplication. You are not going to only win free tickets but more money, that's just gratitude in all parts of your life.

3. UNIVERSAL LAWS

There are natural laws ruling our world.

ABUNDANCE

No matter the nature of the gift, this is abundance, and it's not only about money. What you receive matters, there is energy beyond objects and things. Intention matters. Your reaction matters. When you give something to a child, the reaction is wonderful. Even if it's a simple gift, a toy, or playing at the park: they are just happy, they have *that sparkle*. You must feel the same joy on the inside. When you win a ticket, you want to convince your subconscious mind and celebrate like you won the jackpot or something big for you. You can feel it internally or express it externally, but you have to experience the excitement. Be like a kid and don't take yourself too seriously, your inner child is still there (and never left in case you have totally lost yourself in adulthood). Remember that the more fun you have, the more you are raising your vibration, the more your manifestations will succeed and expand. First, you will manifest small and then bigger and bigger prizes until you got that jackpot.

GRATITUDE

"Whoever has will be given more, and he will have an abundance. Whoever does not have, even what he has will be taken away from him." *(The Holy Bible, Matthew 13:12)*. Whoever has gratitude and appreciation for what he/she already has will be given more, and he/she will have abundance. Whoever does not have gratitude and appreciation for what he/she already has, even what he/she has will be taken away from him. And trust me, it's true because I've experienced it. Some people can be "broke" or lose possessions because they didn't appreciate their gifts in a way, living in scarcity or just "wasting" their blessings, not valuating them. Money is energy. Money comes when it's invited. Money leaves if it's not welcomed. If you don't valorize and appreciate what you have, win, or receive. It can run away from you.

VOCABULARY IS IMPORTANT

You should never use the term "broke". It repels. If you can erase it from your vocabulary, it will change your life in so many aspects. Same for "wasting". Replaced it with the word "investing". You are investing in your health if you buy food. It's self-care if you buy new clothes. You are investing in your health if you go to the gym. You are investing into your education and confidence if you travel. You are investing in your happiness and fulfillment if you go to an art class. You are investing in your education if you pay a coach or take that workshop. You are investing in your future playing the lottery. You are investing in your mental health if you see a therapist, etc.

<u>USE THESE WORDS</u>

- ✧ wasting > **investing**
- ✧ I don't have > **I have**
- ✧ I can > **I already have / am**
- ✧ I will > **I have** or **I am**
- ✧ I hate > **I love**
- ✧ I should > **I am** or **I have**
- ✧ I don't deserve > **I'm worthy**

DELETE THESE WORDS

◆ ~~That's impossible~~

◆ ~~Broke~~

◆ ~~If and Maybe (doubting yourself)~~

◆ ~~I will never / I can't~~

◆ ~~I hope (despair)~~

◆ ~~I don't want (never say that you don't want something)~~

◆ ~~Why does this always happen to me (victim mindset)~~

The Universe doesn't understand the NO. Instead, speak into existence the things you want to manifest. Don't speak about the things you don't want, don't like or hate. Don't say them, Don't write them. The Universe doesn't make a difference with the negation.

QUANTUM PHYSICS

You can't destroy energy. Energy has 2 forms: it either expands or changes its form. What you put in is multiplied. The Universe works with a dynamic expansion. Everything is expanding towards us. It's an attraction-based universe.

THE CONSCIOUS MIND AND THE LOTTERY

The conscious mind can create resistance. It cannot see something that is not possible to its mind, so it can't see the unknown. For your ego it's a game of chance or luck, that's what it sees and what the world shows us. Even if you convinced yourself that playing the lottery is an investment, the ego is going to play and try to make a timeline because your ego lives with time. Your ego says, "I'm not going to be here forever, I need it now!". Your ego believes that you are going to die and not get what you want. This is why we get so pressured with time on our minds, and this is why everyone is running after time everywhere. Now your subconscious knows it will be forever, so there is no concept of time. If it thinks you are here forever, you will be here forever.

UNDERSTAND YOUR EGO

The purpose of your ego is for you to process this world, how to survive, and how to protect yourself, it was developed with the basic necessities for the world around you. You process the entire Universe through your five senses: sight, hearing, smell, taste, and touch. You didn't have to develop these skills to get all this abundance. That's why your mind can't see possibilities and put everything on a pedestal. That's why your ego brings you back down most of the time. Your ego is just trying to protect you against anything that could happen to you. That's why this feeling of security and comfort trapped us in our daily lives. Your ego is protecting you with outdated programs, and it's something that stays inherently into our DNA. It's always going to be like that.

It's up to you to recognize when your ego says that. With the lottery the ego will give you a lot of resistance: from saving your money, from auto-sabotage, "*it's a game of odds and luck and it takes a lot of time to win and it's not going to happen. Look at all these losing tickets, you are the same*". It's up to you to self-correct. It's up to you to take your power back and change your mindsets. Yes, it's a lot of personal work and how much can you convince yourself.

"I've got a free ticket?" Yes, I won the lottery!!!
"I've won 2 dollars?" Yes, I won the lottery!!!
"I've won 10 dollars?" Yes, I won the lottery!!!

4. YOUR POTENTIAL

You have to realize your power.

BUILD YOUR INTUITION

You are going to build your intuition so much that you can use this into your secular life, with your business or money life. Whenever you go and look for these tickets to call you, you are strengthening your intuition. So, they're going to be days when you're going to go in there, and I'm going to show you how. You are guided all the time. If you see someone scratching a ticket, maybe you should buy the same scratch-off. There is nothing by accident. It's all about synchronicities. Anything in your life coming around has a purpose. If you are going to the store, and before you even go to the machine to scan your ticket, you see a scratch ticket on the floor that somebody dropped, that's the one you are going to buy. Many people won that way, including myself. Next rule: never reject a mistaken ticket. If someone chooses the wrong ticket for you, just take it (that's the Universe). You can win $5 million just like that. It happened to me and I won $20,000...like that! A simple mistake for a scratch ticket.

Everything is a simulation game: you can deliberately affect that to win. If it wasn't a game, there would be no way for you to manifest because everything would be set up in a physical way. It just appears that way to us. It's a game within a game. That's also why so many people struggle to manifest. They take it way too seriously. It repels.

I can teach you how to become super perceptive and aware. The Universe is going to throw signs to guide you to pick the right ticket. Don't take anything for granted. You are there,

and you have to be open with the lottery, also remember that coincidences don't exist. There are signs everywhere around you that push you to buy a certain ticket. Playing the lottery is helping you to build your intuition. And now you bring it over to your secular life, and you're going to pick up those great things just like that. If you are open and living in high vibration, you are a perfect candidate for the law of attraction. That's why winners are winning because they are in a high vibe frequency. That's why you are getting the results you're getting because you are approaching this with the right mindset. If you see it as a game, and you have fun...that's the whole point.

Another "game" example that the Universe is showing you: I was buying my ticket and there were places where you can get drive-through tickets. They opened the window and the wind started blowing all the tickets and there was one ticket that the wind just kept flipping and blowing. All the other tickets weren't moving. That was a divine sign from the Universe. I bought it and it was $500 winning instantly. When you start to do that, you become entangled with this concept.. It becomes a sign in your life. Anywhere you're going to go, you're going to see signs about the lottery.

CREATE YOUR OWN NUMBERS

Imagine you are going to pick powerful numbers that call you. For me, it was 47 47, I visualized it (I've seen this number winning). I picked that number and I won over $107,000, straight away. **This is how you collapse your numbers.**

✧ **You can ask your higher self to show you the numbers.** Every night when you go to sleep, you want to say out loud, *"give me the winning lottery jackpot top prize numbers in my dreams"* or any other affirmation that resonates with you. Keep a journal and a pen close to your bed so, when you wake up at night with the fresh numbers you can write them down.

✧ **You deliberately pick and create the numbers yourself.** Relax, meditate, when you reach a higher state you can start to think about any number that comes to your mind. You can follow your intuition. You can choose family dates or something that matters to you. Follow your intuition and what works best for you.

✧ **You can do meditation and write the numbers right after.** You choose the numbers when you meditate and they come to you, repeating *"I just want to see numbers"*. You are not particularly thinking about any numbers, you're just going into meditation, you will see forms, colors, and the numbers shaping themselves.

✧ **You can scan your numbers.** On your daily road, you can allow the Universe to picks numbers for you. When you are driving be aware, you can see a truck that pulls out and has 6 numbers, the receipt at the grocery store, you see numbers repeated... Pick those numbers until you get your 6 numbers if you play Powerball.

Then you can start to play and put those numbers on a slip and collapse them to win. You *intentionalized* to win the game. After you'll open the lottery application on your phone to see the winning numbers. For me it's the Florida Lottery website. If I pick a Mega Million Number, I use visualization and I mentally replace their numbers with my winning numbers, I see myself winning and I see my name next to the winning numbers.

Your subconscious mind does the creative part and thinks that your winning numbers are what's really happening in reality. You have to trick the mind to see what you want to see. Make this visualization a habit. Do this technique when you wake up, before going to sleep when you are daydreaming. It's a powerful tool that works for me because:

1. It's happening in real-time because I'm opening the application on my phone and looking at it. Then your ego gets less resistance because your ego sees that number **superposed**. It's not going to give you that much trouble, and your ego gets confused. Your ego is protecting you so it's better for your ego to feel confusion instead of torment or negativity. The ego is tricked.

2. You change your reality in two aspects: the physical and the mental. Both of them represent the same for your subconscious mind. The physical has the power to affect the mental (action, meditation, visualization, writing, affirmations, saying out loud). To manifest things you have to get your ego on board. When the conscious mind wants the same thing as the subconscious mind it's easier to create. When your conscious mind is in a resistant mode.

You can also photoshop the image and put *your* winning numbers. You can use that image as wallpaper on your phone, you can print it and pin it on the car steering wheel, on your fridge, on the mirror of your bathroom, so you see it all the time. You can look at your phone and do the work mentally too, visualizing and acting AS IF.

The most important thing after this routine, it's pretending you have won. "I just won the lottery. Wait. I just won the lottery !" Your subconscious mind creates and imposed your own reality. Do it and repeat it until you succeed.

Work on yourself, try different techniques, and use the one that works best for you. You have to use the power of your imagination.

My reality is not congruent, your subconscious mind is saying that something doesn't match. Your subconscious is looking for something to match. Somewhere down the timeline, I have to experience winning that lottery. Your subconscious has a different timeline or a different dimension than our regular conscious mind. We have linear time (years and months). You have to get out from that timeline with the lottery, or you will be in a loop. It took me twelve months to manifest a huge amount. For some, it's a long time, but to me, it didn't feel like twelve months. Don't live in the linear time, you just rinse and repeat and stay in the moment until it manifests. If you think *it's too long* or *it will be too late*, (and I know how this part is challenging) remember that these perceptions are illusions of your mind, projected by your ego. When I won it, was the perfect moment.

YOUR MOVIE IS ALREADY MADE

Our brain sees things in three dimensions. We currently live in a higher dimension, it's where everything manifests: you have already won the lottery, more than once, you already got the house, the dream job, the relationship, the clients, the travel, the experience in a higher dimension. According to Quantum Physics, everything is happening right now. You are walking in your own manifestation without perceiving it. Remember that our brains are only three-dimensional, so we were made to perceive up, down, left, right, and we use time as a fourth dimension. When you are **superposing** you are tapping into that dimension already, and then your brain catches up with what you call in. You see yourself already doing it or having it. Our brains are incapable of accessing those higher dimensions in a physical until they come into a three-dimensional world. The minute you put a thought in your head, is the key to letting you know that you have this already manifested. For the subconscious, whenever you put something in your head, you are going to get the feeling (your emotional mind). The reason you get this feeling is because your mind believes it happens.

My subconscious gives me a sign: the feeling in my body that I've already manifested. Even though my brain is in three-dimension, my subconscious mind doesn't access three-dimension, but accesses infinity. So, your subconscious can perceive those higher dimensions. If I have a feeling, that's my subconscious mind giving me a sign, "Mark, you have just already manifested. Otherwise, I wouldn't give you a feeling." Knowing that makes me more determined and just keep more persistent until this matter comes into my 3D world.

TRANSMUTE YOUR FEELINGS

When you have fear, doubt, anxiety, stress, it's something that you don't want. So that's why people always talk against those things because it brings you what you don't want.

To handle fear and doubt you have to understand it's just a feeling that you're experiencing, it's not your reality, it doesn't mean you manifested that. It's linked to survival and with something you can't do, that's the message from your subconscious mind. You have to consciously understand it's your mind picking up on a survival thing. When fear comes in, you understand that it's an illusion. Fear doesn't mean it's happening now. Fear has no immediate impending danger.

When you have fear, show yourself that it's not real. Freeze, stop what you are doing, come back to yourself, and realize it's an illusion. Ask yourself, *"Does that thing I'm just fearing is happening right now?"*. It can. It's impossible it happens right now, because if it was happening right now it wouldn't be fear, it would be dangerous. The feeling of fear is what's keeping you from getting your desires. It's the feeling of this emotion that cripples you because fear itself is invisible. It doesn't exist, it's not real, and it's an illusion. Feeling doubt, feeling fear, feeling anxiety, feeling stress, it's the feeling worry that makes you sick and that's getting you stressed because it's not happening now. Those things are all made up, and that's what keeps us stuck.

It always circles back to one point: being in the now. Now, being in the moment, that's how you get all your answers. That's how you manifest the lottery, by being in the now. When I won that prize that took me one year. If I didn't have my mind checked I'll probably give up a long time ago. Because I was playing every day and my ego would probably say *"Hey man you've been playing all day, it won't happen, give up."* But because I fought it and didn't allow it, I was in the moment and I understood how it worked. And I knew if I keep superposing it, keep doing it, my subconscious gets it. When that number came out, it came out exactly the way I see it in the app, the way I visualized it, the exact same numbers, same day, the same moment of the day.

Your mind is very, very, powerful, much more than you can imagine. You are in those higher dimensions immediately. It's just a matter of what we call "time", what it takes for your brain to bring it to the 3D world: your brain is processing the information, but you can only do it a short amount of time because it's three-dimensional. Higher dimensions are infinite, they're beyond our awareness, so it's naturally going to take your brain some time. When you are superposing, it's already created. When you see higher dimensions, you can't experience, touch, or feel it until it transmutes into your 3D world, where your brain sees it and forms the images and then "wow", then your senses come online, then you have it.

We bless all the people who have purchased this book.
The more you invest in yourself, the more you will receive.
Keep your vibration and frequency high.

Made in United States
North Haven, CT
05 January 2025

64026515R00024